Original title:
The Willow Whimsy

Copyright © 2025 Creative Arts Management OÜ
All rights reserved.

Author: Atticus Thornton
ISBN HARDBACK: 978-1-80567-384-2
ISBN PAPERBACK: 978-1-80567-683-6

Wandering through Green Fantasies

In a land where the breezes tease,
Lively leaves dance with ease.
A squirrel sings a silly tune,
Chasing shadows 'neath the moon.

Bouncing balls of dandelion fluff,
Twirling like a soft little puff.
Frogs in top hats leap and prance,
Inviting everyone to dance.

A rabbit's hat hides carrots galore,
With a wink, he shouts, 'There's more!'
Laughter ripples through the trees,
As shadows play, a breeze does tease.

Giggling flowers in a bright array,
Whisper secrets of the day.
A clumsy bug trips in a spree,
Smiling up, 'Well, that's just me!'

Reflections in a Tranquil Pool

In a pool so smooth and clear,
Frogs wear crowns, and fish cheer!
A turtle twirls in pure delight,
While dragonflies dance in the light.

A stick slipped by with a goofy grin,
"Did you see my last spin?" it chimes.
The lily pads giggle, oh what a sight,
As they play peek-a-boo, morning and night.

The Art of Quietude and Grace

Squirrels gossip in hushed tones,
Debating the best acorn thrones.
With tails like feathers, they prance around,
In a ballet of nutty joy unbound.

The wise old owl acts quite uptight,
But can't resist a midnight flight.
He hoots a tune that's quite absurd,
Making all the other birds chuckle and stir.

Veils of Green in a Sunlit Realm

Beneath the bows, shadows gleam bright,
Where rabbits waltz in sheer delight.
A party of ants with tiny hats,
Strut their stuff, dancing like bats.

"Why no snacks?" the raccoon fumes,
As he rummages through the blooms.
He finds a crumb, holds it high,
And with a smile, sings, "Oh my, oh my!"

The Secret Lives of Breathing Branches

Branches whisper secrets to the breeze,
Tickling leaves like playful tease.
"I swayed left, then swayed right,"
Said one branch, "What a silly flight!"

A family of birds reenacts a show,
With squawks and hops, they steal the show.
The audience giggles, it's quite a scene,
In their leafy theater of vibrant green.

Reflections in Nature's Mirror

In the pond where frogs play chess,
A turtle claims he's quite the best.
He moves with pride, oh what a sight,
But leaps away when things get tight.

The willows nod, they laugh and sway,
Caught in games of night and day.
A squirrel yells, 'I'm winning here!'
As acorns fly with gleeful cheer.

Underneath the laughing trees,
A raccoon hums to buzzing bees.
With every note, the world feels light,
While shadows dance till the moon's bright.

Oh nature's mirror, what a show,
With creatures acting just for show.
Life here is a merry jest,
Where whims and giggles never rest.

Enigma of the Reaching Boughs

The branches reach, they twist and bend,
As if they're waving to a friend.
A crow debates with a nearby cat,
'Who's got more style?' 'Oh, think of that!'

The winds are in on all the fun,
They whisper secrets, just one by one.
A pair of rabbits start to dance,
While daisies giggle at their chance.

In the stillness, laughter rises,
As shadows share their funny surprises.
Each leaf a critic, each breeze a quirk,
Nature's antics forever at work.

Mysteries wrap in a giggly haze,
While critters ponder in a daze.
With every twist, there's much to see,
A riddle wrapped in joyous glee.

Starlit Dreams Above a Canopy

Underneath a starry dome,
A raccoon dreams of a fancy home.
He steals a hat, he steals a shoe,
'Tis quite a life, he thinks, it's true.

A bat swoops low, with a wink and a grin,
'Let's start a party, let the fun begin!'
The owls hoot some gossip from above,
While fireflies light up the night like love.

A swirling breeze invites a dance,
While pine cones fall, they too take a chance.
The giggling branches join in the spree,
As shadows prance like kids wild and free.

Oh, the dreams that twinkle at every turn,
With fields of laughter, we all will learn.
The night is young, the joy is grand,
In this lively and whimsical land.

The Artistry of Nature's Limericks

In a meadow, a flower recites,
With petals waving in funny flights.
It tells a joke that really sticks,
And makes the bees dance in their clicks.

The clouds chuckle overhead, in white,
While butterflies chase with delight.
A snail sneaks up, says, 'Slow it down!'
And yet, they spin like a dizzy clown.

Each brook murmurs a playful tune,
As crickets croon beneath the moon.
With murmurs of mischief in the air,
The grand performance leaves us all in flair.

From daffodils to dandy vines,
Nature crafts smart and silly lines.
In this gallery of merry things,
The laughter lingers, as joy it brings.

Swaying Secrets of the Meadow

In the meadow where giggles grow,
Grass tickles toes, oh what a show!
Fluffy clouds dance in the air,
While butterflies pull off their flair.

Silly rabbits join in the fun,
Chasing shadows just for a run.
Dandelions spin like top hats,
As bees don tiny, buzzing spats.

Dreamy Prospects of Enchanted Boughs

Under branches twisted and thick,
Squirrels perform their acrobatic trick.
With acorns as props they do play,
Nature's circus brightens the day.

Singing birds with a comical tone,
Join the chorus, they won't be alone.
The leaves clap along with delight,
In this whimsical woodland, all feels right.

The Enchantment of Graceful Roots

Roots waltz beneath the unaware,
Fashioning shoes from soil and air.
With every twist, they create a giggle,
As they wiggle and dance, oh how they wiggle!

Fungi in hats, looking quite dapper,
Join the shindig as nature's napper.
Sprightly moss joins in with a cheer,
These charming critters spread so much cheer!

Serenade of the Bend and Bow

Boughs sway gently in harmony,
Singing tunes for all to see.
Trees with grins, a comical sight,
Throwing shadows under the sunlight.

With whispers of breeze and a laugh,
Branches dance a rousing half.
They nod in rhythm, there's joy to be found,
In this merry ballet all around.

Harmony in a Woodland Serenade

In a forest where the trees dance,
Squirrels twirl in a silly prance.
Frogs croak out a tune so grand,
While rabbits clap with tiny hands.

A raccoon juggles acorns with flair,
Chasing butterflies through the air.
The owls hoot with a wink and grin,
As the sun sets, let the fun begin!

Chipmunks burst into a rock band,
Playing music throughout the land.
Woodpeckers join with a flick of the beak,
Creating beats, oh so unique!

The trees sway low with a giggling sound,
As nature's laughter spreads all around.
With every breeze, a chuckle's shared,
In this woodland dance, no one's spared!

Tales from the Swaying Green

Underneath the leafy dome,
A playful gnome calls this place home.
He tells tales of magic and cheer,
While rabbits roll, they kick up their rear!

Mice in tuxedos dance in a line,
As fireflies twinkle like stars that shine.
With every shimmy, every quake,
The trees giggle as branches shake.

A deer with a hat struts with pride,
While squirrels join in for a wild ride.
In this forest, all's merry and bright,
Where even the shadows are laughing tonight!

With every rustle, a story unfolds,
In the sway of the green, where laughter's bold.
Join the fun, let your worries flee,
In this enchanted glen, wild and free!

Enchanted by the Wind's Caress

Dancing leaves in a breeze so light,
Whisper secrets with pure delight.
A butterfly lands on a snoozing dog,
As the frogs croak a joyful fog!

A hedgehog spins with a curious leap,
While the cranky old owl takes a nap, not a peep.
Each branch sways in a comical way,
Like a child playing, come out to play!

Clouds drift low, bringing shadows funny,
As sunbeams sparkle like drops of honey.
With a smile from nature, we just can't resist,
Join in the fun; you won't want to miss!

From babbling brooks to the tickling breeze,
Each moment is filled with playful tease.
Let laughter bubble, let your heart sway,
In this whimsical world where we all play!

A Breath in Nature's Symphony

In the woods where the jesters play,
Trees wear hats in a bright display.
A fox strums leaves like a guitar,
While bees buzz tunes from near and far.

An orchestra of critters is on the scene,
With a raccoon conductor, sharp and keen.
The snail's slow slide is a graceful move,
While the rabbits hop and start to groove.

Clouds above are fluffy and proud,
As a bottomless Skype call shouts loud.
In a leafy hall, all creatures unite,
Nature's symphony plays through the night!

Balloons made of petals float on by,
With a wink and a nod, they wave goodbye.
In this merry melody, hearts take flight,
As we sing along in pure delight!

Flights of Fancy on Gentle Breezes

In the park where whispers play,
Silly squirrels scamper away.
A kite gets tangled, losing flight,
As giggles soar into the night.

Bubbles dance in sunlight's grin,
Chasing shadows, round and thin.
A frog in boots starts to croak,
While a laughing breeze starts to poke.

Laughter blooms like wildflowers,
Tickling noses, brightening hours.
A dog in shades struts with flair,
Wagging his tail, without a care.

Here the world spins on a whim,
Joy on laughter's playful brim.
Each moment twirls, a dance divine,
As fun and fancy intertwine.

Canvas of Light and Leaves

Leaves are painted in shades of glee,
Swirling colors, wild and free.
Sunlight spills like lemonade,
Bouncing off the grand parade.

A painter spills his paint with flair,
Hues of chuckles fill the air.
A moose with glasses poses wise,
While butterflies perform their ties.

Giggling brushes dance and swoosh,
Creating scenes that gently whoosh.
In the laughter, art takes flight,
Crafting joy, banishing fright.

Each stroke a tickle, bright and bold,
Stories in colors yet untold.
The canvas comes alive, it seems,
In the gallery of giggling dreams.

The Solace of Shade and Sound

Beneath the branches, whispers hum,
A squirrel's chatter, here they come.
A snail in shades is sipping tea,
While beetles waltz so merrily.

A picnic spreads with crumbs galore,
Ants parade like they own the floor.
With sandwiches, jokes fly around,
In this cozy place, joy is found.

Grass tickles toes, so soft and green,
In this haven, we laugh unseen.
A turtle nods, oh how wise!
Sharing secrets under the skies.

With every giggle, time takes flight,
Lost in the joy, we feel just right.
In this shade, the world feels grand,
With playful whispers, hand in hand.

Echoing Euphoria in the Grove

In the grove where happiness thrives,
Chirps and chuckles spin like hives.
Frogs are croaking in merry tunes,
While raccoons dance beneath the moons.

A jester's hat on a garden gnome,
Sprinkles laughter to every home.
Tiny feet of children race,
Painted smiles upon each face.

Sticks become swords in epic play,
As giggles chase the clouds away.
Fireflies blink, a bright parade,
In this joyful light, fears do fade.

The trees sway to a silent beat,
And every heart finds a happy seat.
In echoes of joy, all feels right,
Together we dance into the night.

Reveries of the Rustic Realm

In a meadow, cows go moo,
While squirrels dance in shoes of blue.
With flowers laughing in the sun,
Oh, nature's games are so much fun!

The rabbits hop like little stars,
While frogs play drums on rusty jars.
Bumblebees with tiny hats,
Join the waltz with jolly chats.

The sunbeams play peek-a-boo,
As the wind sings a merry tune.
Chasing shadows, a silly spree,
In this realm, we all run free!

When night descends, stars wink bright,
And crickets chirp with sheer delight.
The woodland creatures start their show,
With giggles wrapped in moonlit glow.

Inked in Green: Tales of the Tree Stirrers

There's a squirrel with a paintbrush tail,
Creating art on a windy trail.
With splashes of laughter in the air,
Each stroke whispers a leafy dare.

The acorns roll like tiny cars,
As chipmunks chase beneath the stars.
Their chatter echoes through the trees,
Tickling the leaves, a silly breeze.

An owl wears glasses far too wide,
Sipping tea on a branch with pride.
"Why do you hoot?" a kitten asks,
"Because it's fun! No need for masks!"

Breezes carry tales of cheer,
Of giggling sprites and deer with beer.
In this place, whimsy's the rule,
Each tree's a friend, each root a stool.

Driftwood Dances on the Stream

A piece of driftwood floats along,
While frogs compose a silly song.
The fish all wiggle in the waves,
Partying like they're rock star knaves.

The otters slide with great finesse,
Wearing ties and cute red dresses.
They twirl and splash—a wet parade,
Making ripples in sunshine's shade.

A turtle stomps with clunky shoes,
While ducks in bowties spread the news.
"Join the dance!" the river calls,
As laughter bounces off the walls.

When twilight paints the water gold,
The playful creatures brave and bold,
Join hands and hoot beneath the moon,
In a stream of joy, let's dance till noon!

Sighs of Serenity in Silken Breezes

A breeze whispers soft to the trees,
While butterflies sip tea with bees.
A hedgehog dons a cap so round,
As laughter echoes all around.

The clouds are puffs of cotton candy,
While leaves do waltzes, light and dandy.
A fox in socks juggles acorns,
While winter grumbles; spring adorns.

The daisies giggle, heads held high,
As moths perform a twirl in the sky.
A clamoring chorus of rustle and cheer,
A hidden magic that draws us near.

As stars blink down with a knowing glow,
We dance in shadows where silliness flows.
In dreams of whimsy, we find sweet ease,
In the sighs of serenity and silken breeze.

Nature's Delicate Tapestry

In a field of flowers bright,
A bee zooms with all its might,
It whirls and dives, a clumsy dance,
While petals giggle at its chance.

The sun sneezes, clouds all laugh,
As raindrops play a jolly staff,
A puddle splashes, frogs leap high,
While ants parade beneath the sky.

A snail in sport, it wins the race,
With tiny tendrils, it finds its place,
And grasshoppers jam with thin guitars,
Creating tunes beneath the stars.

So let us laugh beneath the trees,
With nature's quirks, we find our ease,
For every leaf and buzzing bee,
A world of jest, so wild and free.

Serenity in the Softest Sound

A whisper floats through gentle leaves,
The laughter of the breeze deceives,
A squirrel slips, does a little spin,
On branches where the adventures begin.

The brook giggles over smooth stones,
As frogs croon silly, off-key tones,
And crickets chirp in a rhythmic parade,
While shadows of the twilight invade.

A daisies' bloom winks at the moon,
Swaying gently in a garden tune,
The stars twinkle like mischief's eye,
As owls hoot jokes from way up high.

So close your eyes and hear the cheer,
Of nature's antics, ever near,
For in the softest sounds around,
Delight in humor can be found.

Embracing the Evening Glow

As sunset paints the sky so bright,
A cat performs its acrobatic flight,
While fireflies twinkle like tiny stars,
And dance around the funky jars.

The hedgehog rolls down a grassy knoll,
With little giggles, it takes a stroll,
As owls swap tales, where secrets grow,
In this whimsical twilight show.

The wind whispers jokes to every tree,
While shadows of whimsy play carefree,
Beneath the glow of a golden sun,
Nature's humor is never done.

So gather round, the day's last beam,
Join in the laugh, share in the dream,
For every moment in soft twilight,
Happiness abounds in this playful light.

Folklore of the Forest's Heart

In the woods where the critters dwell,
A squirrel's chattering casts a spell,
With tales of nuts and daring feats,
It keeps the forest in joyful beats.

The rabbits dance in a grassy line,
To a rhythm that's quite divine,
While the raccoon, with a gleeful grin,
Tries to juggle berries as they spin.

The ancient trees, they nod along,
To the creatures' laughter and their song,
While mushrooms giggle, hiding in shade,
In this world where dreams are made.

So let us wander through this cheer,
Embrace the jokes that nature steers,
For every heart has room to jest,
In the forest, where we all find rest.

Whispers of the Weeping Tree

Beneath the boughs, a giggle flows,
A squirrel dances, twirls and shows,
It thinks it's suave, a little star,
But trips on roots, oh how bizarre!

With branches swaying, secrets tell,
The tree chuckles, its leaves do swell,
It sways to jokes, the breeze does laugh,
A comedy in nature's path.

When raindrops fall, they tease the ground,
The tree's a joker, never bound,
It splashes puddles, makes a mess,
While critters flee, in sheer distress!

What wisdom lies in tangled hair,
Of leafy crowns with silly flair,
It whispers jokes to those who stay,
To share a laugh at end of day.

Dance of the Silver Leaves

In twilight's glow, they take their flight,
Silver leaves swirl, a dazzling sight,
They prance and twirl, with playful ease,
As if they've danced with giddy bees.

A gust arrives, the leaves collide,
They giggle loud, like kids they hide,
Who knew a breeze could spark such fun,
With nature's laughter, we become one!

They twist and twirl, a merry spree,
Declaring themselves the masters of glee,
While woodland critters pause to see,
This leafy ballet, frolic and free.

Their rustling sings a jolly tune,
As night descends, beneath the moon,
The silver leaves, in dance they stay,
Forever frolicking, come what may.

Echoes Beneath the Boughs

In shadows deep, where laughter rings,
A melody of silly things,
The branches creak, a playful sound,
As giggles echo all around.

A rabbit hops, all eyes aglow,
But trips on roots, oh, what a show!
The echoes bounce, they never cease,
With every stumble, comes more peace.

The wise old owl, with crooked smile,
Watches the commotion for a while,
With wings stretched wide, it joins the fun,
As mischief spreads beneath the sun.

A chorus of chuckles fills the air,
As woodland friends all gather there,
Under the boughs, the fun won't cease,
An endless game, a bond of peace.

Secrets of the Shaded Grove

In shady nooks, where secrets hum,
The woodland critters dance and drum,
With acorns flying through the air,
Their silly antics, quite a scare!

The trees, with laughter, shake their limbs,
As playful shadows twist and skim,
They whisper tales of hasty bees,
Who joke about their clumsy knees.

A turtle joins, so slow it crawls,
While mockingbirds mimic all its calls,
They giggle as they mimic slow,
And chase the breeze, their spirits grow.

In the grove's embrace, fun doesn't hide,
With giggles spreading wide and wide,
They share the secrets, day and night,
In nature's laughter, pure delight.

Memoires of the Muffled Moonlight

In shadows soft, a giggle floats,
The moon hides jokes in silver coats.
A raccoon dances with a sly grin,
While owls debate who'll win the spin.

A firefly buzzes, tries to impress,
"Catch me if you can!" it starts to stress.
A frog croaks out a silly tune,
Underneath the lazy, watching moon.

The breeze whispers secrets, light and thin,
While crickets laugh, it's all in good spin.
A squirrel trips over acorns galore,
And stumbles with a clumsy encore!

When night takes charge, the fun begins,
In a realm where laughter always wins.
With every glance, silliness abounds,
In muffled moonlight, where joy surrounds.

The Lilt of Nature's Gentle Touch

A fluttering leaf, a playful tease,
The breeze begins to tickle the trees.
A chipmunk wears a tiny fedora,
Sipping dew drops like a curious explorer.

The flowers giggle, their colors bright,
In this garden, every bloom's a delight.
A worm in shades of pastel pink,
Sways to melodies, as if it can think.

A gentle swish, the branches bow,
Nature chuckles, takes a little vow.
To keep the joy flowing all around,
Where every corner has laughter found.

Sunshine spills like syrupy fun,
Playtime's not over, it has just begun.
With every laugh, my heart takes flight,
In nature's arms, everything feels right.

Glimmers of Gold in Twilight's Arms

As day gives way to the giggling night,
Golden horizons dance in delight.
A squirrel in shades of sunset glow,
Practices jump-rope, putting on a show.

The clouds wear blush, like cheeky sprites,
While laughter spills from fading lights.
A butterfly flutters with a wink,
Tickling petals, skirts of pink.

With shadows stretching, tricks abound,
In twilight's embrace, joy can be found.
A spider spins webs of sparkly dreams,
In the laughter of stars, glowing beams.

Twilight giggles, it's far from shy,
As crickets tune up their nighttime lullaby.
With every twinkle, a playful tease,
In this golden hour, hearts find their ease.

Interludes in a Verdant Playground

In the realm where laughter takes its flight,
A field springs forth in colors so bright.
Bouncing bunnies trot in a race,
Chasing their tails in a merry embrace.

A ladybug dons her party dress,
As ants march in single-file finesse.
The daisies clap with a gentle cheer,
Inviting all critters to come near.

A swing of vines brings the fun alive,
While kittens tumble, they twist and dive.
Each leaf knows secrets of countless pranks,
As nature winks and gives her thanks.

In this playground, silliness reigns,
Through whispers of breezes, joy it sustains.
Every blade of grass, a partner in jest,
In verdant laughter, we find our rest.

Beneath the Veil of Verdant Grace

In a garden where giggles grew,
The flowers wore bonnets, it's true.
Bees buzzed with a comical hum,
While butterflies danced, oh, how they'd come!

Squirrels donned shoes that were bright,
Chasing the shadows in playful flight.
Rabbits played tag with the breeze,
Each leap a laugh, a giggle, a tease.

Laughter hung on each leafy sprout,
As the sun winked down with a shout.
Nature's own jesters in bloom,
In this merry, enchanted room.

So if you wander this whimsical place,
Join in the fun with a smiling face.
Underneath the green, all is fine,
With whimsy and joy, your heart will shine!

Fables from the Fluttering Fronds

Once a fern told tales with flair,
Of a snail who danced without a care.
With rhythm so smooth, none could believe,
He twirled through the leaves, as light as a breeze.

A chipmunk chimed in, voice full of glee,
Said, "I've got acorns, come dance with me!"
They jived past the flowers, two merry men,
Fables of laughter, again and again.

Whispers of wisdom from branches above,
Where the pigeons plot with no hint of shove.
Their chatter brings chuckles, oh what a bow,
As they share little secrets we'll never know.

So gather your friends, lift your voice high,
Let the stories of nature make spirits fly.
In this playful world where laughter is free,
Every tale told dances joyfully!

Mysteries of the Moonlit Branches

In the shadows where owls hoot,
A raccoon wore a ninja suit.
With stealthy steps and a twitching tail,
He sneaked through the grass, quite the tale!

A moth joined in, wings grand and wide,
"Let's explore the night!" he cried with pride.
They wandered together, a curious pair,
Spooking the crickets who stood in despair.

Moonbeams laughed as they danced about,
Tickling the leaves, filled with sprout.
Whispers echoed from the night's gentle lace,
As stars twinkled down, sharing their grace.

So heed the call of the night's sweet sound,
In hidden spots, fun can be found.
Under moonlit branches, secrets delight,
Where whimsy and laughter take flight!

The Aesthetic of Arcane Elegance

In a realm of charm, where giggles grow,
Wands made of twigs put on quite a show.
Fairies twinkled with mischief at hand,
Making magic that's oh-so-grand!

A pot of laughter brewed by a brook,
With jokes that could even make stones shook.
Each splash a sound of crisp delight,
In an artistry woven with pure light.

Sass from the shadows, a wise old toad,
Belted out sonnets on the lightened road.
Pond lilies nod in gleeful acclaim,
As frogs leap along, spouting their fame.

Embrace the whimsical, the quirky, the fun,
For life's a dance, a race to outrun.
Let joy be your guide in this splendid scene,
Where laughter and magic weave evergreen!

Harmonies Wrapped in Leafy Lullabies

Underneath the branches wide,
Squirrels dance with silly pride.
Chasing shadows, swift and spry,
Bouncing like a bumblebee in the sky.

Rabbits giggle in a line,
Waltzing as if by design.
While the brook hums a tune,
Gloriously under the bustling moon.

Rustling leaves join the cheer,
Whispers for all woodland near.
Twisting, turning, they declare,
Nature's party floating in the air.

Even the owls laugh with glee,
Holding secrets of the tree.
In harmony, they make their way,
Singing loud till the break of day.

Whimsical Threads of Nature's Loom

Twirling vines in a vibrant dance,
Each leaf dressed for a merry chance.
The windy whispers play their role,
Stitching magic from a giggling soul.

Silly bugs with no intent,
In a silly parade, they are content.
A butterfly, a quirky sprite,
Flutters by to join the light.

An acorn cap becomes a hat,
Worn by a playful, prancing cat.
As laughter echoes through the glen,
A mischief brewed by bird and hen.

Threads of laughter, spun with cheer,
Nature's quilt that wraps us here.
Each moment wrapped in fun and glee,
A patchwork stitched by you and me.

Beyond the Bark: A Story Untold

Once upon a time, so cheeky,
A raccoon with a heart so freaky.
He wore a sock upon his head,
Claiming it was fashion spread.

An antelope pranced through the glade,
With sparkling shoes, they danced and swayed.
Each step was a jest, a light-hearted leap,
While laughter echoed, never to sleep.

In the hollow of a twisted tree,
The tales of the woodfolk run wild and free.
Each critter shared a funny line,
Of blunders painted with love divine.

So if you wander on this path,
Expect the whispers of nature's laugh.
For stories bloom where fun takes root,
In every bark, a silly hoot.

Serenades at Twilight's Embrace

As twilight drapes a golden shawl,
Creatures gather for a ball.
With twinkling eyes and cheerful sound,
In every nook, joy is found.

Bunnies hop to a jovial beat,
While owlets share their tasty treat.
The whispers of leaves join the song,
Inviting all to sing along.

With fireflies flickering like stars,
They dance on air from near to far.
Wings abuzz with giggles sweet,
Carrying tales on tiny feet.

At dawn, when laughter fades away,
The woods will welcome another day.
Through night's embrace, the silliness plays,
In nature's heart, where fun always stays.

Gentle Tears of the Stream

In the brook, a splash and giggle,
A fishy joke, it makes us wiggle.
Ducks quack loud, they crack a pun,
As ripples dance and play with sun.

A turtle slips on slime so slick,
With a puffed-up laugh, he does a trick.
Leaves rustle softly, sharing jest,
While frogs croak tales of their best quest.

Old stones chuckle, mossy and spry,
As breezes tease the clouds up high.
Nature's stage, with laughter bright,
In watery winks, all feels just right.

The pebbles giggle in their own way,
While fish do cartwheels, making a play.
Waves of joy tickle roots below,
In this happy stream, all troubles go.

Elegy of the Whispering Trunks

Tall trees wear grins in the soft breeze,
With branches swaying, they dance with ease.
Knobbly knees giggle at tickling light,
As squirrels attempt their acrobatic flight.

A woodpecker knocks on a trunk with cheer,
While owls drop wisdom both witty and clear.
Breezes hum tunes that tease the bark,
As shadows play tag from noon until dark.

Leaves join the chorus, a rustling joke,
As wise old oaks share puns in smoke.
Their laughter rings through the woodland green,
In this grand forest, fun reigns supreme!

With roots entwined, they tell their tales,
Of ticklish branches and weathered gales.
In every whisper, a chuckle is found,
Among these trunks, joy knows no bound.

Dance of the Dappled Sunlight

Sunbeams prance on leaves so bright,
They skip and leap, a joyful sight.
Dancing shadows join in the game,
With giggles echoing Nature's name.

Butterflies flutter, each twist a jest,
They tease the flowers, never at rest.
Petals shake hands with the morning air,
Spreading laughter, a fragrant affair.

The daisies chuckle, the roses grin,
As sunlight winks, they spin and spin.
Glowing softly, all nature beams,
In this funny dance of sunlit dreams.

The playful light twirls above,
Casting a spell, a wink from love.
As day drifts on, and shadows grow,
Joy and laughter in every glow.

Tendrils of Twilight's Embrace

Twilight whispers, secrets to share,
As night creeps in with a playful air.
Stars start twinkling, a cosmic prank,
As shadows stretch on the riverbank.

Crickets chirp with comedic flair,
In a concert hall of evening air.
Fireflies blink, their lanterns bright,
Sending silly winks to the stars at night.

The moon rolls in with a chuckling beam,
Casting a smile on the evening's dream.
With each soft flicker, joy is found,
In twilight's laugh, all hearts abound.

As tendrils of night wrap the land,
The world creates a wonderland.
With giggles weaving through the trees,
In the embrace of night, we feel the breeze.

Sweets of the Verdant Dance

In the breeze, the leaves do sway,
A jumpy frog sings all day.
With candy blooms that smile so wide,
A candy-coated world, a bizarre ride.

Charming critters flaunt their attire,
While ants are juggling, oh, how they tire!
Sugar-spun laughter fills the air,
As bees breakdance without a care.

The clouds above chuckle and tease,
While squirrels host parties with nuts and cheese.
Each twig a dance floor, no time to stop,
For nature's a circus, let's pop and hop!

A cherry pie rain, sprinkle it sweet,
Every heartbeat's a tap of the feet.
So join the whimsy, don't hesitate,
In this candy land, let's celebrate!

Stories Written in the Flickering Shadows

Underneath the moon's bright grin,
Mice weave tales that begin with sin.
Shadow puppets prance and play,
While owls wink—'tis a funny fray.

In the dark, a raccoon schemes,
Juggling acorns and wild dreams.
A cat narrates, with flair and style,
While fireflies dance, illuminating each smile.

Every crack and crevice hums,
With giggles and pitter-patter drums.
The night is alive with secrets galore,
Where laughter echoes and spirits soar.

A grand stage set by the stars above,
Where every critter is filled with love.
So listen closely, don't miss the show,
For in shadows flicker, the laughter flows!

Vignettes of an Urban Refuge

Amidst the chaos of cars and cries,
Pigeons tap-dance, oh how they fly!
A park bench thrives, a gossiping place,
With squirrels sharing tales, full of grace.

Graffiti blooms in colors so bright,
While streetlamps wink, embracing the night.
The city hums a tune of delight,
As hipsters skateboard, under neon light.

A hotdog stand serves dreams on a bun,
With mustard twist, it's all just fun.
A lazy cat sprawls, a monarch supreme,
In this urban jungle, life's but a dream.

So cherish the bustle, the laughter and play,
In every corner, joy finds its way.
For in this refuge, wild adventures bloom,
Life's a comedy, dispelling all gloom!

The Comfort of Canopied Shelter

Under branches swaying with glee,
A party's brewing with ants and a bee.
With leaf hats on, they dance in a row,
An anthem of chuckles, in shadows they flow.

The picnic blanket is quite a sight,
With snacks that giggle in pure delight.
Every crumb's a comical prize,
As tiny squirrels plot mischief in disguise.

The canopy whispers secrets untold,
Offering shelter from storms so bold.
Together they joke as rain starts to pat,
Sharing their warmth, not a moment to chat.

So grab your friends, and join in the fun,
In this leafy haven, everyone's spun.
With laughter as currency, and joy for each hour,
Beneath this green wonder, we flourish and flower!

Laughter in the Lattice of Light

In the garden where shadows play,
A squirrel steals acorns, what a day!
The flowers giggle in the breeze,
As bees buzz by with silly pleas.

A cat in a hat struts with flair,
Jumps on a ledge, without a care.
A rabbit hops, tripping on leaves,
While a gopher dances, oh, how it weaves!

The sun's a jester, bright and bold,
Tickling flowers, stories untold.
A ladybug rolls on a daisy crown,
The world spins round in a whimsical town.

Graceful Shadows on the Water

Ripples giggle where ducks parade,
While fish flip-flop, a splash cascade.
A frog croaks jokes from his leafy throne,
While dragonflies zoom like they've grown!

Whispers ripple amongst the reeds,
As shadows sprout from tree's good deeds.
A turtle tumbles, finds his shell,
And giggles with joy, oh what a swell!

The sun winks down, a cheeky sprite,
While clouds drift by, like cotton polite.
This unexpected splash of fun,
Brings laughter where the wild things run.

Tides of Time in Twisted Roots

Beneath the old tree's tangled hair,
A wily fox spins tales with flair.
The roots are dancers, lost in the groove,
Their sways and twists get all to move!

A snail races slow, oh, what a champ,
While ants hold a circus, a mini camp.
Laughter bounces from branches above,
As vines entwine in a silly love.

The moon peeks in, a curious guest,
Watching antics, it can't help but jest.
Time ticks on, yet here we stay,
In this garden of laughter, come what may.

Serene Dreams of the Swaying Canopy

Up high, the leaves whisper soft dreams,
Of dancing shadows and moonlit beams.
A raccoon wears stars like a fancy tie,
As butterflies chase him, oh me, oh my!

Woodpeckers knock, setting the beat,
While fireflies twinkle, oh, what a treat!
Crickets chirp their nightly song,
In the canopy dance, where all belong.

A breeze tells tales of nights gone by,
As owls hoot softly, beneath the sky.
In this realm where dreams take flight,
Serene and silly, under starlit light.

Choreography of the Gentle Wind

The wind starts to twirl, oh what a sight,
Dancers on leaves, in sheer delight.
Swaying to tunes that none can hear,
Whirling and twirling, full of cheer.

A gust gives a nudge, it's a playful tease,
Polka with petals, tumbling with ease.
The branches shake hands, a leafy embrace,
Each waltz and jig, leaves a grin on each face.

Watch out for the squirrels, they want in too,
Trying their best in a furry zoo.
With each little leap, they slip and slide,
It's a party out here, come join the ride!

Oh, the giggles of grass as it tickles the toes,
Every little rustle, a tale that grows.
In the ballet of nature, we all shall blend,
A caper of joy, where laughter won't end.

A Reverie in the Rustling Leaves

Breezes tease branches, making them dance,
Whispers of secrets caught in a trance.
Leaves giggle as they flutter and fall,
A raucous riddle, a light-hearted brawl.

A caper of colors, spinning and bright,
Leaves put on a show, oh what a sight!
With a puff of wind, they leap to the sky,
Daring the clouds to join in their fly.

Acorns roll out, with mischief afoot,
Chasing the shadows where laughter is put.
Nature's own jesters, in this leafy domain,
Who knew that the forest could be so insane?

When twilight approaches, and shadows play,
Leaves still are laughing, the sun fades away.
In this merry madness, we too can sway,
Join in the festivity, come what may!

The Whimsy of Dusk's Softening Glimmer

As daylight winks, a curtain descends,
Critters emerge, in delightful blends.
A chirp here and there, a giggle takes flight,
In the softening glow, mischief feels right.

The fireflies' flickers, a cheeky parade,
Lines of bright dancers, in darkness displayed.
They poke at the night, with a yellowish spark,
Bringing the glow to the whispering park.

The moon cracks a joke, shining overhead,
"Look at those shadows, so easily led!"
While crickets compose their nighttime tune,
Dusk plays the fool, under the smiling moon.

Oh, join in the laughter, as darkness sets in,
Nature's own folly, let's spin and spin.
With silly old stars, and chuckles in tow,
This merry old nightshow will steal the show!

Elysian Dreams in the Breeze

When breezes giggle through a meadow bright,
Dreams dance like dandelions caught in flight.
A tickle of laughter rolls over the plain,
Nature's own daydream, wild and untamed.

Each whispering flower joins in the game,
With petals that flutter like laughter proclaimed.
Bees buzzing jokes, while butterflies glide,
In this fanciful world, joy cannot hide.

Puffballs tumble, with a mind of their own,
Spinning and sprawling, the seeds are now sown.
With each playful gust, a chuckle we hear,
In this land of whimsy, there's naught to fear.

So let's join the revels, beneath sky so wide,
In a kaleidoscope of joy, let's reside.
For in these sweet moments, we find our reprieve,
In the laughter of nature, we learn to believe.

Whimsy in the Weeping Green

In gardens where the shadows play,
A squirrel stole my lunch today.
He danced around with stolen fries,
A heist beneath the sunny skies.

The flowers giggled, petals shook,
As he munched on my favorite cook.
I chased him 'round, a comical sight,
A chuckle shared in morning light.

A butterfly joined in the chase,
As if to join the funny race.
Together they twirled, a grand parade,
While I just stood, my plans delayed.

And so, beneath the weeping trees,
Laughter danced upon the breeze.
Who knew a snack could spark such joy?
A picnic thief, a playful ploy!

Odes to Breezes and Brambles

Through the path of prickly brambles,
I strolled with friends, caught in gambles.
A gust, it whispered, 'Join the fun!'
We fell like leaves, a jolly run!

The bushes chuckled, full of glee,
As we dove down, all wild and free.
Our laughter echoed, nature's song,
To breezes swift and days so long.

A worm with shades, quite dressed to thrill,
Complained of sunlight, said "Chill, chill!"
We shook our heads, not one to care,
For joy was found in sunny air.

So if you wander, heed this tale,
Where brambles twist and breezes sail.
Grab a friend and share a laugh,
In nature's playful photograph!

Light Filters Through the Veil of Leaves

Amidst the trees with leafy veils,
Where sunlight dances, laughter trails.
A cat with glasses read a book,
While squirrels plotted, shadows shook.

The sunlight grinned, a playful tease,
As leaves would rustle in the breeze.
A rabbit hopped, a curious gaze,
In this comical sunlit maze.

An acorn fell, a fateful drop,
It landed plop on a turtle's top.
He blinked in shock, then gave a sigh,
"I swear it's sunny, not July!"

So wander here where laughter grows,
And time's just play, as nature knows.
In filtered light and shadows tall,
The world is funny, after all.

A Soliloquy Beneath the Sky

Here I sit, on mossy ground,
In quiet thought, but giggles found.
A crow cawed loud, with much to say,
A feathered critic of the day.

The clouds above, they whispered low,
A game of tag, a shadow show.
They chased each other, fluffy fluff,
While I just sighed, my thoughts were tough.

A butterfly flitted, quite the tease,
It landed near, just to wheeze.
"Is this a drama? A comic play?"
I laughed aloud, what a funny day!

And so I ponder, beneath the blue,
Life's quirky dance, exciting too.
Let's toast to laughter, a charming pie,
In this whimsical soliloquy, oh my!

Refuge of the Enigmatic Embrace

In a nook where shadows play,
A gnome in slippers waltzes sway.
With squirrel pals, they spin around,
Tickling roots beneath the ground.

A wizard's hat fell with a flump,
The toads all laughed, they did a jump.
Ice cream cones made from petals bright,
Stir up giggles, a silly sight.

Beneath the branches, mischief brews,
Where dandelions share the news.
The raccoons hold a midnight feast,
And rumor has it, they are beast!

The moon peeks in, a cheeky grin,
As frogs start up their ribbit din.
In this embrace, let laughter ring,
For nature loves its silly fling.

Tides of Time in the Canopy

Breezes whisper tales of old,
As acorns dance in hats of gold.
A wise owl blinks, "Who's up for fun?"
"Let's play hide-and-seek 'til we're done!"

The branches stretch like arms in cheer,
Inviting all, both far and near.
When a fox in spectacles prances,
You know for sure, the forest dances!

Beneath the leaves, a party brews,
With tiny chairs and mushroom stews.
A funky beat from ants on cue,
Entices all to join the brew!

As stars come out, the laughter grows,
In this canopy, joy freely flows.
Swinging from vines, they twirl away,
Kicking up dreams at end of day.

Dreams Caught in Vines and Tendrils

Tendrils twine like fingers tease,
A snail in shades does as he please.
Fairies knitting dreams with flair,
While crickets chirp, "Do take care!"

Amongst the vines, a hedgehog found,
A treasure trove beneath the ground.
Marshmallow clouds in a jelly jar,
"Let's take them all, we'll travel far!"

With giggles shared amongst the crew,
A pickle dance, they joined anew.
The sun dips low, its colors blend,
While prickly pals do twist and bend.

At twilight's gate, the mischief swells,
As everyone rings tiny bells.
In this realm where whimsy plays,
Tomorrow's laughter softly sways.

The Calm that Dances with the Wind

Whispers ride on twirling leaves,
A jester swings, delight he weaves.
In breezy hugs, the daisies chuckle,
While butterflies wear sparkly buckle.

A dandy bee with stripes galore,
Buzzes jokes by the garden door.
With every tickle, blossoms bloom,
As giggles spread around the room.

The sun dips down with playful tease,
Tickling toes of the swaying trees.
A family of owls hoot in glee,
"What a show! Come join us, see?"

As shadows stretch and stars ignite,
They dance along 'til dawn's first light.
In this calm with wind's soft song,
Laughter hums, and hearts belong.

Nature's Gentle Lullaby

In the shade where the branches dance,
Leaves tickle the air, a leafy prance.
Squirrels giggle, chasing their tails,
While the breeze hums softly, spinning tales.

Bumblebees buzz with a merry tune,
Dancing with flowers, from sun to moon.
A butterfly flutters, oh what a sight,
Whispering secrets from morning to night.

Grassy blades serve as slip-n-slide,
Where frogs leap and croak, full of pride.
Shadows wiggle, play peek-a-boo,
Nature's antics, a grand review.

So come take a nap beneath this flair,
With giggles and chuckles filling the air.
For in this world, both quirky and spry,
The laughter of nature, oh me, oh my!

Enchantment of the Whispering Winds

A gentle breeze whispers secrets bold,
As ants embark on journeys of gold.
Poppies nod their heads in delight,
While dandelions dance, graceful in flight.

Breezy chuckles through the tall grass roll,
Tickling the trees, making them whole.
Clouds pass by sporting fluffy hats,
While gophers play poker, oh what chitchats!

The rustling leaves join in the fun,
In a game of hide and seek, they run.
Each gust carries laughter far and wide,
As the world spins together, side by side.

So let's listen close to the wind's sweet sound,
For in its giggles, joy can be found.
Every whisper holds magic, I dare claim,
Nature, my friend, is never quite the same!

Songs of the Softly Swaying Sapling

A little tree sways, oh what a sight,
With leaves that giggle and twirl in flight.
Roots tickle soil, a dance so divine,
Nature's little comet, oh how it shines!

It dreams of growing, reaching the sky,
With branches that wave, whispering "Hi!"
Its buddy, the bumble, hums a sweet tune,
As the sun spills laughter all afternoon.

Dewdrops sprinkle sparkles, giggling so light,
While snails take their time, savoring the night.
Each beat of life sings a silly refrain,
In the playful chorus, we all entertain.

So skip with the sapling, take joy in the jest,
For growing up funny is truly the best.
Let nature's tunes keep your spirits high,
In the garden of laughter, together we fly!

Chronicles of the Ancient Arboreal

In the realm of giants, stories unfold,
Wise old trees stand, their secrets untold.
Bark cracked with laughter, rough and sassy,
With owls perched nearby, sullen yet classy.

They chuckle of centuries past and gone,
Of busy squirrels and the dawn's first yawn.
Crickets chirp in rhythm, a quirky choir,
As shadows stretch long, never to tire.

Mossy tales weave through the fabric of time,
Spinning yarns so silly, they bubble and rhyme.
Acorns drop down like playful little bombs,
As nature blooms forth with its wise, leafy charms.

So gather around, let us ponder and play,
With stories of laughter that dance through the day.
For in the embrace of these gentle giants,
The chronicles live on, forever defiant!

The Magic of Soft Shadows

In a garden of giggles, shadows play,
They dance on the ground, in a joyful ballet.
A leaf takes a bow, then trips on a twig,
The sun laughs aloud, 'Oh, that was quite big!'

Beneath a grand branch, a snail wears a hat,
With a lingering gaze, he chats with a cat.
They ponder the mysteries of wandering breeze,
And compare tales of naps spent up in the trees.

Elysium Amongst the Trees

The trunks wear their hats, made of shining green,
With squirrels as tailors, it's quite the scene.
A dance-off ensues on this woodsy runway,
As branches sway wildly, in splendid dismay.

The woodpecker winks, with a tap-tap-tap sound,
While ants join the cha-cha, all over the ground.
A butterfly giggles, in polka-dotted flight,
As blossoms erupt in colors so bright.

The Symphony of Swaying Grace

A jaunty young breeze starts a ticklish spree,
Whispers and giggles float high through the leaves.
The dancers all sway, in tuneful embrace,
As laughter erupts from their leafy dear space.

Chirping crickets swing, conductors of cheer,
While fireflies flicker, like stars drawing near.
The harmony swells, a riotous sound,
In this wild symphony, where fun is compound.

Tales of a Whispering World

In this land of soft murmurs, where secrets take flight,
A frog with a microphone croaks into the night.
He tells of grand feasts under moonlit beams,
Where raindrops are cupcakes, and laughter, it gleams!

With a wink and a nod, a wise owl takes flight,
To share more of tales that light up the night.
Among roots and remains, stories bounce all around,
In this whimsical world, joy and humor abound.

Puzzles in the Bark of Time.

A tree with quirks, oh what a sight,
Knots twist and turn, left and right.
Secrets written, ancient and wise,
A riddle in bark, to spark surprise.

Squirrels giggle, their tails in knots,
Chasing shadows and silly thoughts.
Who carved the names up high and low?
A mystery waiting in every row.

Branches whisper, tickle and tease,
Nature's pranks, done with ease.
A leaf drops down with a playful spin,
While all the others just wear a grin.

Time plays tricks in this wild place,
Each twist and turn a funny face.
As laughter rings through the swaying limbs,
The riddle's song forever swims.

Whispers of the Waving Branches

In the breeze, the branches sway,
They gossip and chatter throughout the day.
Leaves play catch with a cheeky gust,
Telling tales that go beyond trust.

A robin's song, a woeful tune,
As it trips over a croaking rune.
The branches wave, a quirky cheer,
While the blooms chuckle, all loud and clear.

A squirrel's dance, on a narrow ledge,
Bumbling along the green hedge.
With flaps of wings and a fluttering sight,
The whole tree laughs, what a funny flight!

Under the sun, a comic show,
Nature's antics put on a glow.
The whispers echo, soft and bright,
In a world where laughter takes flight.

Lullabies on Gentle Breezes

Softly sung by the breeze that plays,
A lullaby drifts through lazy days.
The flowers nod to the sleepy tune,
While bees buzz in a dreamy swoon.

Mice giggle under the starlit sky,
Dreaming of cheese, oh my, oh my!
The breeze wraps round like a comfy quilt,
As laughter stirs, no room for guilt.

Crickets join in chirping so sweet,
In a rhythm that quickens little feet.
Each note a giggle, a tickling tease,
Where sleepyheads sway with the trees.

And when the moon paints shadows wide,
The whispers of joy cannot hide.
A night of dreams, fun like no other,
Just singing soft with nature's mother.

Shadows Dance Beneath the Canopy

Beneath the green, the shadows play,
A dance of giggles, bright and gay.
The wind spins tales, twirls around,
Where laughter sings, joy knows no bound.

Frogs take leaps like silly clowns,
As butterflies flit in colorful gowns.
The sunbeams sneak through leaves above,
Flashing smiles as they show their love.

The ground is alive with jigs and prance,
Creatures all join the laughter's dance.
In this haven where shadows blend,
Funny antics never seem to end.

Soon the stars tag in the show,
With twinkles and winks, they steal the glow.
Together they weave a tapestry bright,
Where whimsy reigns in the soft moonlight.

Cascades of Silvered Leaves

Leaves tangle in a dance, quite absurd,
With squirrels plotting heists, that's the word.
Branches sway like dancers in a spree,
A leaf slips, and a laugh sets it free.

Nature's giggles echo in the air,
A tinted backdrop, light as a feather.
The breeze whispers secrets, oh so sly,
As acorns tumble, aiming for the sky.

Each flutter of leaf, a comical jest,
They shimmy and shake, never at rest.
In this playful whirl, fun takes its stand,
With each silvered flake, the dance is grand.

A twig bows low, mock-saluting the day,
While critters grin in humorous play.
Amongst all this laughter, take your cue,
Join in the frolic, there's joy for you!

Moonlit Murmurs in the Grove

Under the moon, the shadows collide,
Whispers of giggles, nature's delight.
Bats swoop and dive, like acrobats bold,
In a play of light, the night stories told.

Crickets partake in a symphony bright,
A riddle of chirps that lasts through the night.
But watch for the owl with plans of a jest,
Who breaks out in laughter, all in good jest.

Frogs croak their tunes, like singers well-laced,
Each ribbit a punchline, no need to be chased.
The breeze joins the fun, rustling leaves low,
An unexpected tickle where moonbeams glow.

Amidst the ogling oaks, a chuckle is born,
Laughter at midnight, a night full of charm.
So waltz in the grove, be part of the dream,
Let humor and nature blend in one beam!

Echoes of a Soft Embrace

Huggable branches spread wide and warm,
Like grandma's embrace, a comforting charm.
Laughter cascades from the tip of each leaf,
In whispers of joy, like a gentle thief.

The wind, a rumor, tickles the bark,
A comedy act that ignites the park.
A gust brings the giggles, a tickle, a gasp,
As branches sway softly, in nature's clasp.

Dandelions scatter, a cheeky affair,
As whispers of wishes float into the air.
Each yearning for laughter, hope wrapped in glee,
Like nature's own jesters, wild and free.

So slip 'neath the canopy, share a good joke,
Under the foliage, where spirits invoke.
Each echo a giggle, a light in the sway,
Join in the embrace, let your heart play!

The Poetry of Nature's Sway

Nature scribbles laughs on the blank sky,
With clouds that pounce, oh my, oh my!
Sunbeams write verses, a light-hearted play,
While flowers burst forth in colors of gay.

The babbling brook sings, a merry refrain,
Splashing and crashing on stones with disdain.
A ticklish embrace from the river so sly,
With fish making faces, as time passes by.

Brush of the wind sings joy in a race,
Pulling the grasses to join in the chase.
Together they frolic, with laughter so wide,
Unfolding the stories where humor collides.

Each twist of a stem, each swirl of a tune,
Beckons to join in, beneath the bright moon.
So dance with the whispers, be light and be free,
In the poetry written by nature's decree!

Flickers of Firefly Fantasies

In the dark, they dance and twirl,
Tiny lights in a nighttime whirl.
They tease and flicker, shine so bright,
Nature's jesters, what a sight!

Glow and wink in a friendly game,
Catch one quick, oh! What a shame.
They giggle soft, like little sprites,
Playing tricks on summer nights.

With their flashes, they try to say,
"Join our merry, silly play!"
But chase them fast, they're quick as a breeze,
Leaving behind a laugh with ease.

In the end, the stars join in,
Winking back with a cheeky grin.
A show of light, a fleeting fun,
Fireflies' dance has just begun!

Clusters of Dreams in Hanging Knots

Beneath the boughs, where secrets hide,
Laughter mingles with the tide.
Tangles of thoughts, both silly and sweet,
In dreaming knots, they wiggle their feet.

Up high, the thoughts dangle and sway,
Whispers of mischief as they play.
Like kittens trapped in yarn's embrace,
Chasing shadows, a jovial race.

In each cluster, a giggle grows,
A tickle of dreams in soft repose.
Hanging on branches, they bounce and leap,
In a world where joy is never cheap.

Amidst the branches, they frolic and weave,
Laughter echoes, hard to believe.
For in these knots, a playful spree,
Where clusters of dreams dance wild and free.

A Tapestry of Golden Sunbeams

Sunlit threads weave through the air,
Golden whispers without a care.
They tickle petals, kiss the leaves,
A merry burst that never grieves.

In the fields where laughter flows,
Sunbeams paint the earth with woes.
They giggle as they slip and slide,
Racing down with gleeful pride.

Each beam a story, bright and bold,
Tales spun from moments young and old.
They trip on shadows, dance in glee,
Creating giggles, wild and free.

When the day dims and night draws near,
Sunbeams wink, "We'll be back, dear!"
Their tapestry glows, a golden stream,
Filling our hearts with warmth and dream.

Musings of the Moonlit Meadow

Under the moon, the critters prance,
In the meadow, they take a chance.
Bunnies hop and badgers trot,
In shadows deep, they weave a plot.

With each leap, a chuckle rings,
As the night air playfully sings.
A dance of whimsy among the grass,
Where silly thoughts wander and pass.

The old owl chuckles from a tree,
"Join the fun, come dance with me!"
Stars above blink in delight,
Mischief sparkles in the night.

Whispers of giggles float so free,
In the moonlit glow of harmony.
For under this sky, so wide and deep,
Even laughter fails to keep.

www.ingramcontent.com/pod-product-compliance
Lightning Source LLC
Chambersburg PA
CBHW071853160426
43209CB00003B/532